FOR BEGINNERS

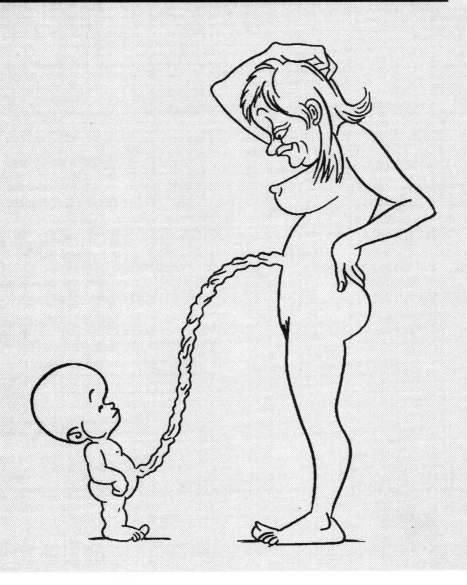

WRITERS AND READERS PUBLISHING, INC.
P.O. Box 461, Village Station
New York, NY 10014

Writers and Readers Limited
9 Cynthia St.
London N1 9JF
England

•

Text Copyright: © 1994 David Brizer
Illustrations © 1994 Ricardo Castañeda
Cover Illustration: Ricardo Castañeda
Cover Design: Terrie Dunkelberger

This book is sold subject to the condition that it shall not, by way of trade or otherwise, be lent, re-sold, hired out, or otherwise circulated without the publisher's prior consent in any form of binding or cover other than that in which it is published and without a similar condition being imposed on the subsequent purchaser.

All rights reserved. No part of this publication may be reproduced, stored in a retrieval system, or transmitted, in any form or by any means, electronic, mechanical, photocopying, recording, or otherwise, without prior permission of the publisher.

A Writers and Readers Documentary Comic Book
Copyright © 1994
Library of Congress Catalog Card Number: 94-060329
ISBN # 0-86316-169-3 Trade
1 2 3 4 5 6 7 8 9 0

Manufactured in the United States of America

Beginners Documentary Comic Books are published by Writers and Readers Publishing, Inc. Its trademark, consisting of the words "For Beginners, Writers and Readers Documentary Comic Books" and the Writers and Readers logo, is registered in the U. S. Patent and Trademark Office and in other countries.

Table of Contents

Why This Book?...1
Why A Baby?..4
Society vs. the Baby...7
How to Make A Baby..16
Baby Unfolding: Fetal Development...21
Illness During Pregnancy...34
Maternal Drug/Alcohol Use..37
Monitoring the Pregnancy...39
Complications of Pregnancy & Birth..41
Labor..45
Birth...55
The First Few Days: What Do I Do?...63
Womb With A View: The World from Baby's Point of View................64
Infant Behavior...68
Infant-Parent Bonding..71
Soothing the Newborn..72
Diapers...75
Baby Talk...76
Baby Psychology..77
Breast or Bottle?..79
Feeding..102
Watching Baby's Growth..106
Abuse: Physical, Emotional, & Otherwise.......................................108
Crying..110
Teething...114
Building A Better Baby: Nature vs. Nurture....................................115
Sleeping...122
History: Baby's Point of View...124
Is Baby Ill?...126
Shots...131
What Kids Need—and What They Don't...132
Playtime..134
Babyproofing...138
Babysitters..146
The Toddler...150
Glossary..153
References..156

You were once a baby.

Maybe you still are.

At one time or another, *every one* of us was a baby.

And hopefully during that time you were, well, *babied:* swaddled, and cooed at, and spoiled, and generally adored.

ANYONE WHO HATES CHILDREN & DOGS CAN'T BE ALL BAD.
—W.C. FIELDS

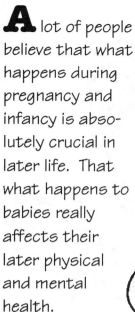

A lot of people believe that what happens during pregnancy and infancy is absolutely crucial in later life. That what happens to babies really affects their later physical and mental health.

If so, then it's important to know exactly what takes place during this short but eventful period: how the baby gets there; how it grows and develops; and what factors help or hinder the transition to childhood.

Why do people have babies?

Why *not?*

Because having a baby is irreversible.

Familiarity breeds contempt—and children.
—Mark Twain, *Notebooks*

Because having a baby is expensive—

not only in terms of money but in terms of time and energy and especially in terms of emotional investment.

Ideally, having a baby is a lifetime commitment to another (new) human being.

> There was an old woman who lived in a shoe,
> She had so many children she didn't know what to do;
> She gave them some broth without any bread,
> She whipped them all soundly and put them to bed.
> —There Was An Old Woman

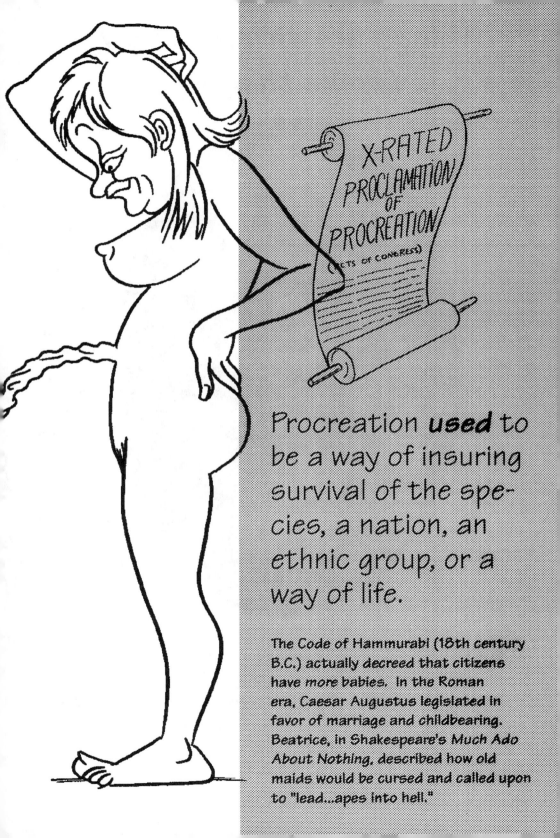

Procreation **used** to be a way of insuring survival of the species, a nation, an ethnic group, or a way of life.

The Code of Hammurabi (18th century B.C.) actually decreed that citizens have *more* babies. In the Roman era, Caesar Augustus legislated in favor of marriage and childbearing. Beatrice, in Shakespeare's *Much Ado About Nothing*, described how old maids would be cursed and called upon to "lead...apes into hell."

Things are different now (some things.)

People (some people) have more options these days: improved methods of birth control, and lifestyle alternatives to parenthood (so maybe having babies is not a universal instinct.)

WE PROBABLY DON'T WANT YOU

A quota on babies—maximum, two per couple—has been enforced for decades in China. Women in India were given free transistor radios as an incentive to undergo voluntary sterilization.

New pressures—increased cost of living, decreased global resources—give greater pause to the would-be parent of today. These days not having a baby, or adopting an unwanted one, are more likely to promote the survival of the human race.

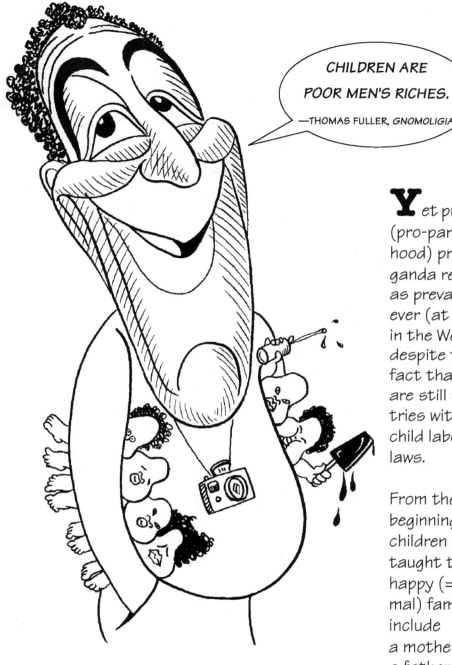

Yet pronatal (pro-parenthood) propaganda remains as prevalent as ever (at least in the West) despite the fact that there are still countries without child labor laws.

From the very beginning, children are taught that happy (= normal) familes include a mother, a father, and two or more kids.

WHEN I GROW UP I'M GOING TO BE A GRANDMOTHER

Helene Deutsch, a psychoanalyst (but probably not a feminist!) characterized pregnancy as the "direct fulfillment of the deepest and most powerful wish of a woman." (*The Psychology of Women.*)

Simone de Beauvoir (*The Second Sex*) disagrees:

"That the child is the supreme aim of women is a statement having precisely the value of an advertising slogan. Some women should not have children."

According to **Sigmund Freud**—bless his departed sexist soul—reproduction was the woman's primary role in life. Women sought pregancy in order to symbolically incorporate and keep the penis (*penis envy.*)

Margaret Mead: You got that one wrong, bub. Men have *womb* (Venus) envy!

Finally, I've got MY own!

Despite all the hype, modern (or is it postmodern?) Western society is curiously *ambivalent* about babies...curiously unwilling to make the necessary sacrifices to ensure the comfort and health and well-being of these creatures that we convince ourselves we treasure so much.

> HE HAD GROWN UP IN A COUNTRY RUN BY POLITICIANS WHO SENT THE PILOTS TO MAN THE BOMBERS TO KILL THE BABIES TO MAKE THE WORLD SAFER FOR CHILDREN TO GROW UP IN.
> —URSULA K. LEGUIN, THE LATHE OF HEAVEN.

52% of the U.S. labor force are women. Yet the struggle for reasonable measures like work leave and adequate day care has only begun (57% of U.S. day care workers earn less than poverty level wages.)

People have babies...because they don't think about it until it's too late.

Or: people have babies because they want a baby,

or: they like or love babies,

or: because they cannot come up with a good enough reason not to have one.

...WHEN THE BOUGH BREAKS THE CRADLE WILL FALL, AND DOWN WILL COME BABY CRADLE AND ALL...

Like many decisions in life, the decision to have a baby is often made on a feeling level.

LITTLE CHILDREN ARE STILL THE SYMBOL OF THE ETERNAL MARRIAGE BETWEEN LOVE AND DUTY.
—GEORGE ELIOT. ROMOLA

People like to believe that *pleasure* is the point of having children.

But in indigent or expanding populations (Indians in Guatemala, or Mormons in U.S.) children become a major source of expendable cheap labor.

How do people have babies?

Contrary to popular belief, getting pregnant isn't all that easy.

Conception requires that the male gamete, or *spermatozoa*, not only make its way through the vaginal canal and cervix, but that it penetrate and merge its genetic message with the mother's egg cell.

WHERE IS ARTIFICIAL INSEMINATION WHEN YOU REALLY NEED IT?

TO THE OVUM

(The dance of the parents' chromosomes, with its awesome complexity and even more awesome result—a baby—is more fully described in *DNA for Beginners*.)

Consider it from the sperm's point of view.

The sperm's pilgrimage to the egg is a long journey (the equivalent distance in full scale human terms would be from New York to Chicago.) And the competition to get there is...stiff. The average male ejaculate contains some fifteen million sperm, each a fierce contender for the egg.)

Of the millions of sperm in each ejaculate, only 300 to 1000 actually make it to the ovum (egg cell.)

The woman *ovulates* (releases an egg from the ovary) once a month; it is only then that conception can occur.

Mishaps can and often do occur. The monthly cycle may be disrupted, and the egg may not be released. Or the egg may implant somewhere other than the uterus; fertilization outside the uterus can lead to ectopic pregnancy, which can be life threatening for the mother. Some sperm (up to 15%) are damaged and fertilization with one of these may result in a non-viable embryo.

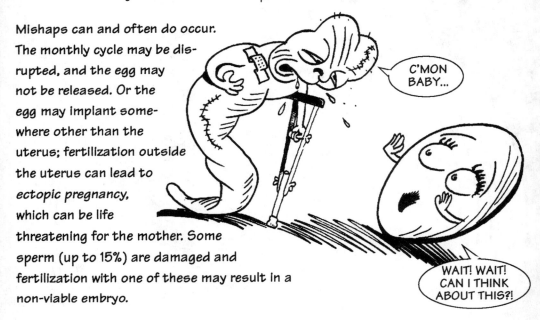

Sad to say, too many women are unable to choose motherhood freely. Many women are not free to decide what is to become of their bodies and lives once they become pregnant.

Up to forty per cent of pregnancies are non-viable and result in spontaneous abortion or miscarriage (usually very early, in the first four to six weeks); the only evidence that this has happened may be a late and/or unusually heavy menstrual flow.

***I**mmaculate conception* has not yet been explained by science.

(see our forthcoming volume, *Hoax and Hearsay for Beginners,* for more on this.)

The fusion of the sperm's and egg's DNA results in a single cell, now containing the full complement of thirty two chromosomes.

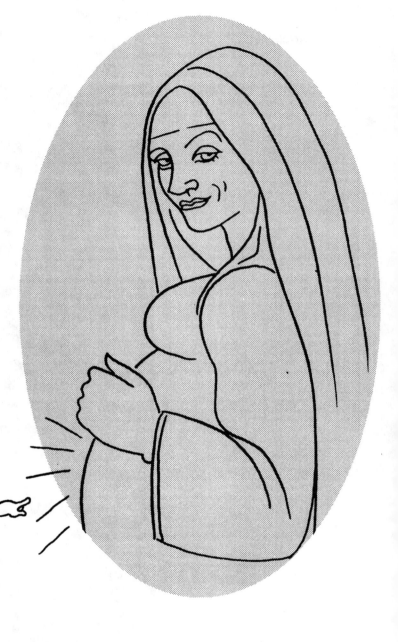

A remarkable sequence of events then follows.

Good things come in small packages; or,

you must have been a beautiful blastocyst.

Q: What *do* Michael Jackson, Madonna, and Schwarzenegger have in common?

A: Like the rest of us, they each started out in life as a zygote.

The **zygote**, the primordial cell containing the combined genetic information from both parents, is *undifferentiated*, but not for long. A finely orchestrated sequence of cell division, migration and adhesion results in specialized cells that will eventually become specific body organs and tissues.

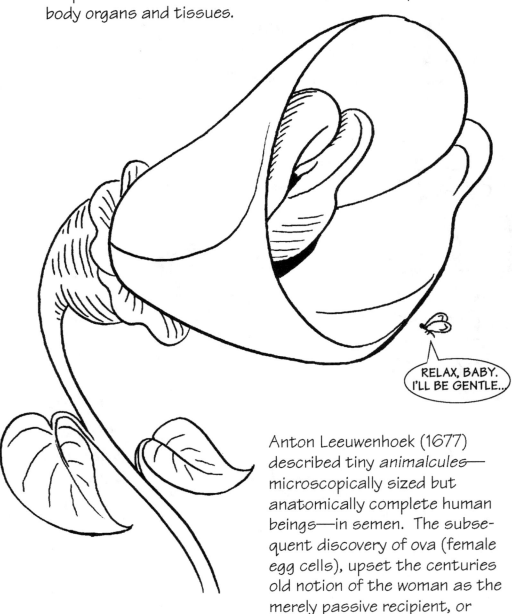

RELAX, BABY. I'LL BE GENTLE...

Anton Leeuwenhoek (1677) described tiny *animalcules*— microscopically sized but anatomically complete human beings—in semen. The subsequent discovery of ova (female egg cells), upset the centuries old notion of the woman as the merely passive recipient, or fertile soil, for the man's seed.

Centuries of superstition held that male 'seed' was precious, vital... and in the absence of conception, sinful to spill (you would go blind, or insane, or grow hair on your palms). There was no corresponding belief for women. (Never forget, Men have written history...)

For millenia, the act of conception remained the same:

Woman + Man = Baby.

It is only very recently, with the introduction of artificial fertilization and genetic engineering, that we can manipulate the stuff of life itself.

I MISS BABIES...

With further increases in cell size and number, the zygote becomes a *blastocyst*, which firmly implants itself in the lining of the uterus. Five days after conception, the blastocyst gives rise to the inner cell mass (destined to become the *embryo*) and the *placenta*, the complex nest of cells that protects and facilitates exchange of nutrients, oxygen, and carbon dioxide between mother and developing baby.

You Are What You Eat
or Drink
or Smoke

The embryonic period (from conception to 8 weeks) is one of frenetic yet superbly organized activity. During this time, the developing organs are extremely sensitive to *teratogenic* (birth-defect causing) influences such as alcohol, drugs, and certain infectious diseases.

...Not to mention the extremely debilitating effects of poor nutrition. Millions of babies worldwide still suffer the consequences of inadequate maternal calorie and vitamin intake. Impoverished or low income groups have more low birth weight babies. (Eighteen per cent of babies in developing countries are low birth weight babies.)

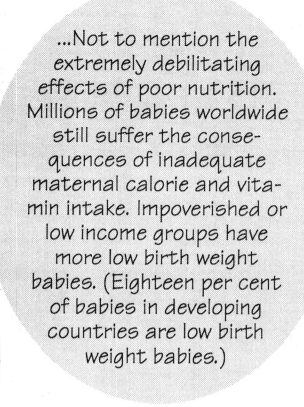

MEN ARE GENERALLY MORE CAREFUL OF THE BREED OF THEIR HORSES AND DOGS THAN OF THEIR CHILDREN.
—WILLIAM PENN

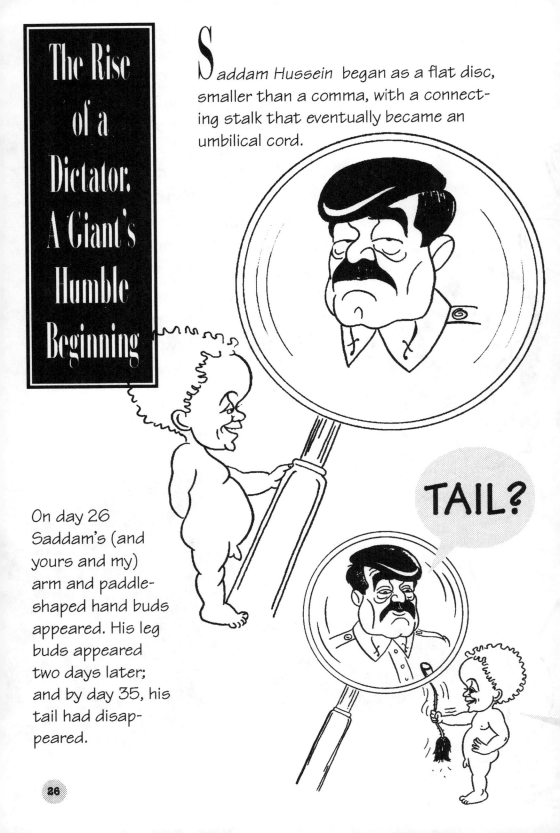

Ontogeny recapitulates phylogeny, meaning that the embryo's development (*ontogeny*) which takes place in stages, retraces the evolutionary sequence (*phylogeny*) from single celled creatures to humans.

At one stage for example, the embryo has a full set of gill slits, much like our phylogenetic ancestor, the fish.

THAT'S RIGHT; TAIL!

By the end of the embryonic period (eight weeks), all major systems and external features are either present or have started to develop.

The fetal period extends from week nine on to term (=delivery.)

> As I in hoary night stood shivering in the snow,
> Surprised was I with sudden heat which made my heart to glow;
> And lifting up a fearful eye to view what fire was near
> A pretty Babe all burning bright did in the air appear.
>
> —Robert Southwell (16th century), *The Burning Babe*

OH! HE'S GOING TO BE SUCH A CUTIE!

Joseph Stalin's mother could feel his tiny movements within her belly by week 18. This is also the time when his fetal heartbeat could be heard.

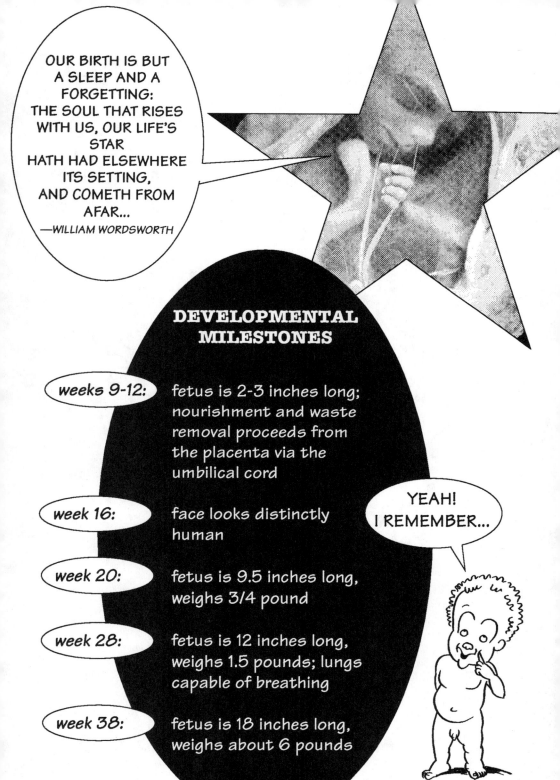

By the 25th to 28th week of gestation, *Ronald Reagan's* eyes had opened.

YEAH... I GUESS THEY ARE OPEN...

Even more importantly, his (and yours and my) lungs could function...

Life outside the uterus could now be sustained.

WOMB WITH A VIEW:

Life Inside the Uterus

WHEN EACH COMES FORTH FROM HIS MOTHER'S WOMB THE GATE OF GIFTS CLOSES BEHIND HIM.
—Emerson, *Conduct of Life*

OBSERVATORY OF THE EXTRAUTERINE WORLD

It's no wonder they make such a fuss about coming out.

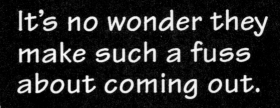

The baby's environment is dark, secure, all enfolding; room service, in the form of a steady supply of life-giving nourishment from the placenta, is available twenty four hours a day. The fetus can twist and turn or loll comfortably about, weightlessly supported by the surrounding amniotic fluid. Baby hears and feels the reassuring sounds of mother's heart beat, the rhythmic peristaltic churning of her viscera, the gentle surge of her blood flow. External sounds like music and voices (and gunshots and sirens) are likewise perceived by the fetus.

THERE'S TROUBLE IN PARADISE: WHEN THINGS GO WRONG

No one would complain if every newborn arrived on time, the happy healthy product of a full term uncomplicated pregnancy and delivery.

But pregnancies and deliveries can have problems.

Exposure of the fetus (particularly during the first trimester) to physical trauma, certain infectious diseases, and most if not all drugs—including prescribed drugs, alcohol, and tobacco—may result in gross or subtle damage to the unborn child.

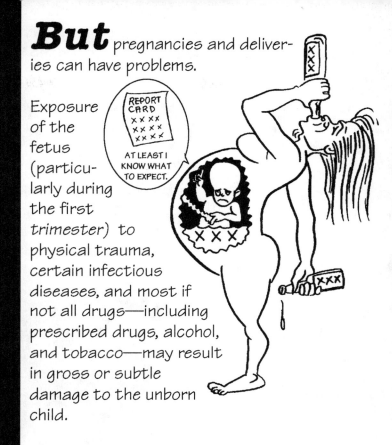

No one has *proven* that emotional turmoil and upset for the mother affect the developing fetus.
Still, maternal stress causes hormonal changes which undoubtedly reach the fetus.

Don't worry, be happy!

is good wisdom for expectant mothers.

Maternal illness in general, and exposure to certain infections in particular, can have little consequence for the fetus...

or

can be catastrophic (or even fatal.) Which is why adequate prenatal care, including childbirth classes for the parent(s) and regular visits with the obstetrician, are crucial.

Some systemic illnesses in Mom that can affect the unborn need careful medical monitoring from the pregnancy planning stage right up until delivery:

hypertension (high blood pressure)
diabetes
thyroid disease
rheumatoid arthritis
lupus
heart disease
kidney disease
liver disease
sickle cell, other anemias
syphilis
HIV/AIDS

Pre-eclampsia, or toxemia of pregnancy, a condition that can arise in a previously healthy pregnant woman, is characterized by new-onset diabetes and high blood pressure. Medical monitoring and management of this (usually) self-limited disorder is critical for the safety of mother and baby alike.

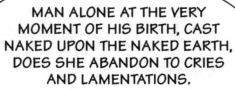

MAN ALONE AT THE VERY MOMENT OF HIS BIRTH, CAST NAKED UPON THE NAKED EARTH, DOES SHE ABANDON TO CRIES AND LAMENTATIONS.

—Pliny the Elder *Historia Naturalis*

Often, fetal exposure to infectious disease occurs 'silently',

without any symptoms or awareness on mother's part. Baby may pick up the illness as she passes through an infected birth canal.

Of particular concern is maternal/fetal contact with rubella, toxoplasmosis, cytomegalovirus, herpes, measles, tetanus, and HIV; these can cause spontaneous abortion, birth defects, low birth weight, and severe illness in the newborn.

Assessment of risk and advisability of vaccination and other precautions should be discussed with the doctor.

> EAT NO GREEN APPLES OR YOU'LL DROOP,
> BE CAREFUL NOT TO GET THE CROUP,
> AVOID THE CHICKENPOX AND SUCH,
> AND DON'T FALL OUT OF WINDOWS MUCH.
> —Edward Anthony, *Advise to Small Children*

"GERMS GERMS GO AWAY COME AGAIN ANOTHER DAY..."

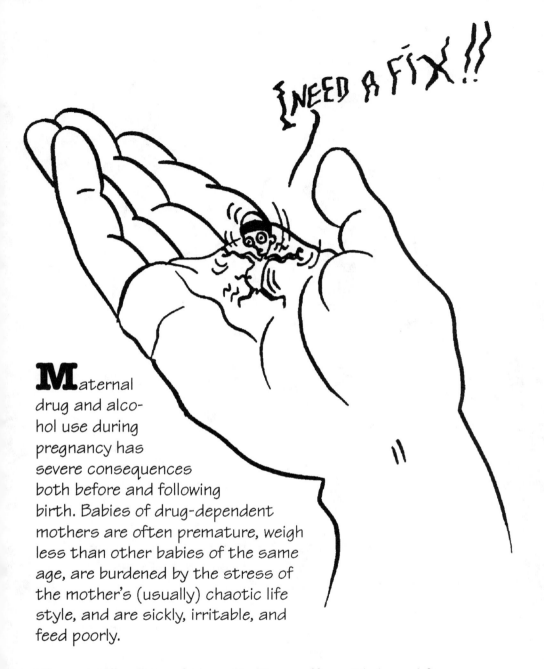

Maternal drug and alcohol use during pregnancy has severe consequences both before and following birth. Babies of drug-dependent mothers are often premature, weigh less than other babies of the same age, are burdened by the stress of the mother's (usually) chaotic life style, and are sickly, irritable, and feed poorly.

Worse still, many of these babies suffer withdrawal from whatever drug mother was abusing. Although some babies catch up later on, many (*crack babies*, for example, and those with *fetal alcohol syndrome*) will struggle with problems like birth defects and mental retardation for the rest of their lives.

Some doctors feel that light drinking (a glass or two of wine, or beer) is not only harmless, but may be positively beneficial because of its relaxing effect.

Most birth defects, or *congenital malformations,* are of unknown cause.

Possible teratogenic culprits include chemical or electromagnetic pollution, and multifactorial insults such as prenatal exposure to environmental toxins *plus* infectious agents.

Other birth defects have a known genetic cause. Genetic counseling and sophisticated pregnancy monitoring such as *amniocentesis* and *ultrasonography* can detect abnormal chromosomes and fetal development. Conditions like *Down's Syndrome* (extra chromosome 21) and defective limbs or vital organs can be picked up in this way.

Amniocentesis

involves the extraction of amniotic fluid through the abdominal wall by syringe. The fluid can then be examined for the presence of blood, *meconium* (waste matter from the fetus), and chromosome abnormalities. This procedure is recommended in situations where there is increased risk for congenital abnormalities (i.e., advanced maternal age, previous children with birth defects.)

With **ultrasound**, reflected sound waves emitted from a flat probe (no needles involved in this test) placed on the pregnant woman's abdomen yield actual images of the fetus. Doctors and parents-to-be can get a direct look at baby-on-the-way, including his or her bone structure, beating heart, and for those who wish...genitals. (The 'pink or blue' decision can be made months ahead of time!)

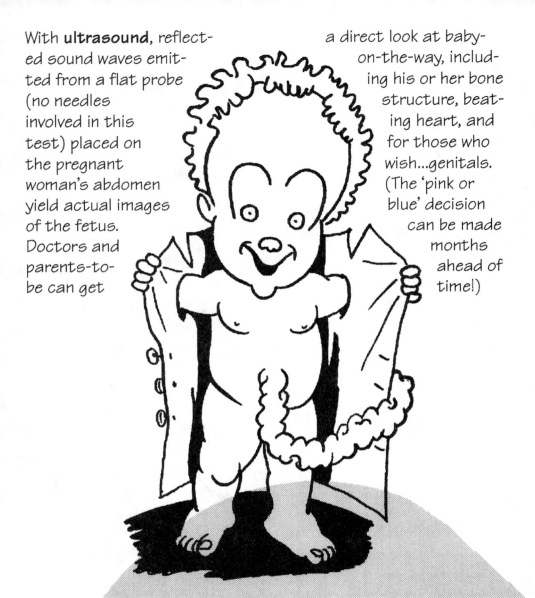

Genetic counseling is useful in families with known hereditary diseases such as hemophilia, sickle cell disease, Huntington's disease, muscular dystrophy, and others.

When a House is Not a Home

On occasion, there are problems with the placement or positioning of the developing fetus.

FINGER OF BIRTH-STRANGLED BABE, DITCH-DELIVERED BY A DRAB.
—SHAKESPEARE, MACBETH

With *placenta previa* the placenta sits between the fetus and the cervix, effectively blocking its exit (when the time comes) from the womb.

In umbilical cord **prolapse,** the emerging baby can be strangled by the umbilical cord. Fortunately, adequate prenatal care, together with ultrasound and other diagnostic techniques, can detect these complications and lead to lifesaving interventions such as *version* (manual repositioning of the fetus while still in the uterus) and, when necessary, Caesarian section.

Premature separation of the placenta from the uterine wall occurs in **abruptio placentae.** Spotting (vaginal bleeding) may occur during these and other problem situations in pregnancy, and should be reported to the obstetrician immediately.

Sometimes baby gets it wrong, and tries to enter the world ass backwards—the so-called **breech** presentation. Ideally, the baby should emerge head first—the fetal pelvis and legs are the widest body parts and don't easily fit through the birth canal unless preceeded by the head.

LET ME TRY FROM THIS SIDE...

EXIT

BUSTIN' LOOSE

History records and celebrates extreme experiences—Hannibal crossing the Alps, the landing of the Allied forces in Normandy on D-Day, the arrival of humankind on the moon. Undoubtedly you have your own milestones as well (learning to walk, learning to swim, getting married are some possibilities that come to mind).

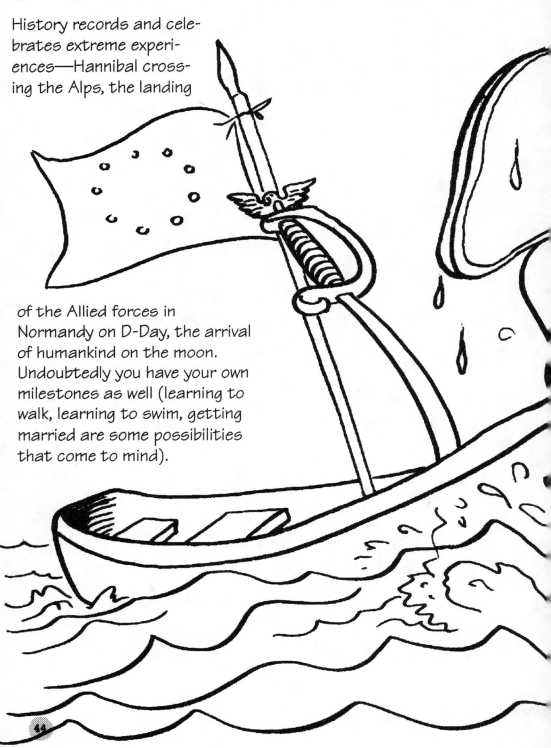

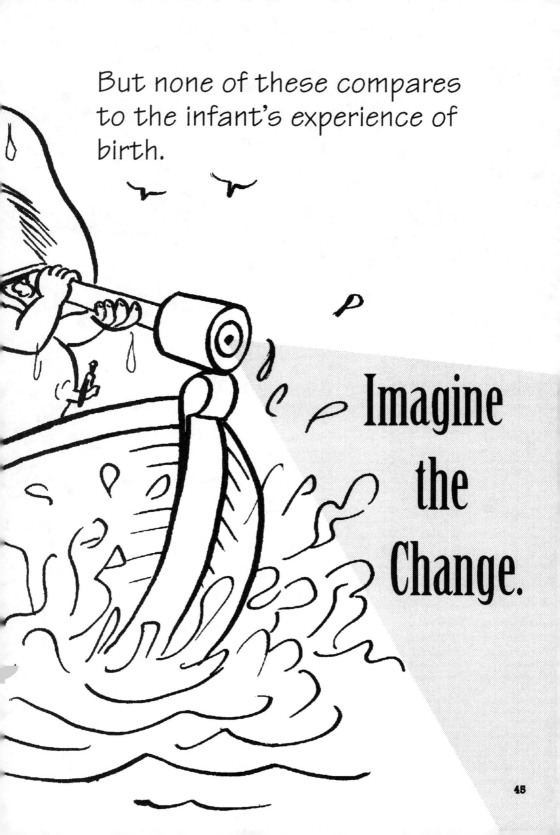

But none of these compares to the infant's experience of birth.

Imagine the Change.

Imagine the warm, darkened soothing nest transformed over the course of a few hours into a bubbling, churning cul-de-sac, wracked by increasingly powerful muscular contractions.

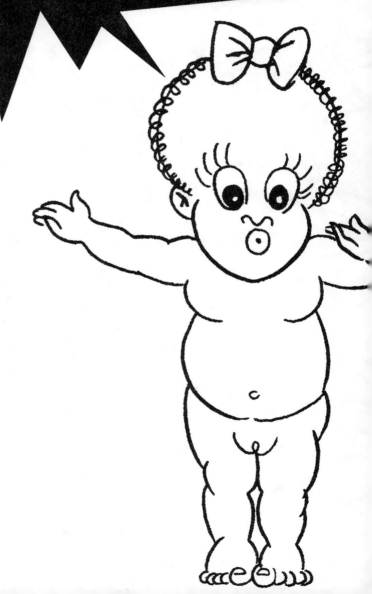

And finally it happens.

And depending on where it happens,

> you find yourself in a cold chrome-and-steel operating room, inhaling the strange odor of disinfectant; you find strange masked and gowned beings peering down at you, handling you, *doing things* to you...
>
>> or you find yourself in a quiet, gentle space, in a warm bath perhaps, or laid upon the yielding softness of your mother's belly.

Up until very recently, childbirth took place at home and was handled by midwives, who specialized in delivering babies. In many non-industrialized, non-Western parts of the world, childbirth is still primarily attended by families, friends, and non-physicians.

GREAT WITH CHILD, AND LONGING... FOR STEWED PRUNES.
—SHAKESPEARE, MEASURE FOR MEASURE

THAT'LL BE THE DAY

Which is good, inasmuch as it promotes community and sharing of the joy and responsibilities of having a baby. But not so good when serious obstetrical problems develop.

Some parents opt for a middle course. Fathers, for example, are increasingly involved these days in the birth of their children.

Mothers and fathers attend birthing classes (Lamaze, others) together so that mother's partner can provide front line assistance—physical as well as emotional—to her during labor and delivery.

The Seven Labors

Labor typically begins as a series of mild *contractions*, often perceived by the woman as a sensation of lower abdominal cramping.

What's actually happening is that the woman's body is undergoing a series of intense changes, hormonal and physiologic and otherwise, that will result in the separation of placenta and fetus from the womb and eventually birth.

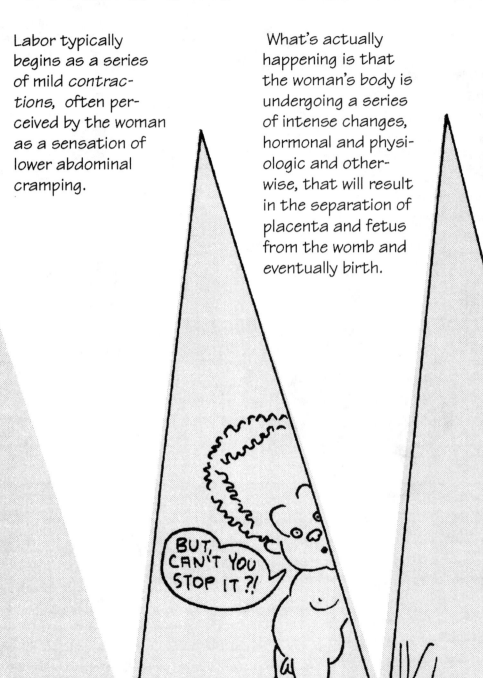

# of HERcules

Once the process starts, there's no going back.

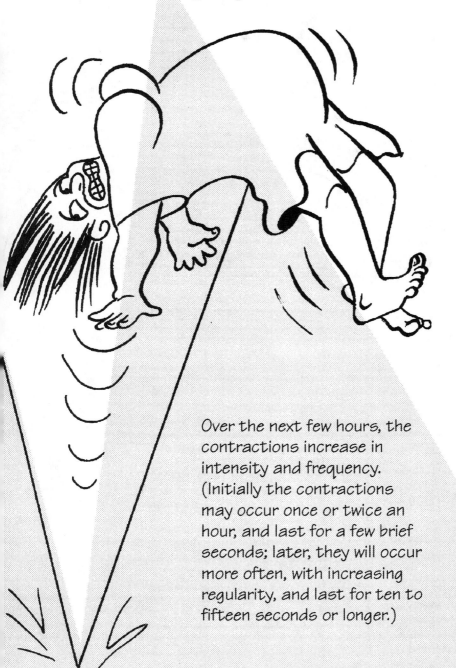

Over the next few hours, the contractions increase in intensity and frequency. (Initially the contractions may occur once or twice an hour, and last for a few brief seconds; later, they will occur more often, with increasing regularity, and last for ten to fifteen seconds or longer.)

At some point during this cascade of events, the woman will break her water. This takes place when the amniotic sac ruptures, releasing some of the amniotic fluid. Breaking water is a sure sign that baby is on the way.

HEY!! WHERE DID MY BATH GO?

As labor proceeds, the woman's cervix *dilates*, opening more and more widely to accomodate baby's imminent passage. The extent of dilation is another index of the progress of labor, with full dilation achieved at 10 centimeters.

Some women have a long, difficult labor, especially if this is the birth of her first child. In hospital settings, under the care of an obstetrician, the expectant mother may be given *oxytocin (pitocin)*, a hormone which amplifies the strength of uterine contractions.

Women (and their doctors) are divided on the issue of 'natural' vs. medically assisted childbirth.

Some feel that labor and delivery should be allowed to proceed at their own pace, and that the woman should be fully aware of her sensations as the process unfolds. In recent years more expectant parents have chosen to move the birthing process out of the hospital and back into the home.

> HURRY UP MOM!! GET ME OUT OF HERE!

Women who find the contractions too painful may insist on anaesthesia; epidural anaesthesia, administered by needle into the spinal canal, temporarily numbs all sensation from the waist down, but allows the woman to be completely awake and to participate fully in the birth.

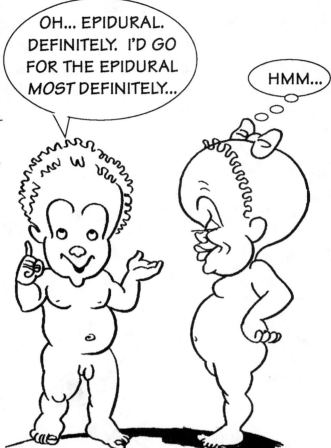

When baby appears, his or her connection to mother, the umbilical cord, is tied and severed.

With the first breath (with or without a slap) baby steps into the world.

YOU'RE HISTORY! I'M OUTTA HERE!

Ye are better than all the ballads
That ever were sung or said;
For ye are living poems,
And all the rest are dead.
—Longfellow, *Children*

LOVE'S LABOR LOST

What about abortion? Or pregnancies that miscarried, that didn't make it to term? The collective grief involved here is perhaps only matched by that surrounding the death of the infant, or of the mother during birth...Which tragically enough is *not* just a thing of the past.

It is estimated that the annual toll of pregnancy-related deaths runs to one half million women worldwide. Native populations in Third World countries routinely practice emotional distancing—'death without tears'—in anticipation of the loss of their young.

Improved social conditions mean reductions in infant mortality... so unlike previous generations, many parents of today can afford the emotional luxury of bonding to their babies.

NOT ALL BABIES ARE CREATED EQUAL

Baby doctors rate the newborn's overall health with an APGAR score, which assesses factors like muscle tone and circulatory competency.

Newborns' health problems may result from complications such as prolonged labor (which can literally tire out both mother and baby) or *abruptio placentae,* in which premature separation of the placenta from the womb compromises oxygen supply to the fetus.

In high risk or life-threatening situations the obstetrician may choose to bypass the birth canal and deliver the baby by *Caesarian section* (surgical removal from the abdomen.)

There has been a dramatic increase in the use of this procedure in the last several decades, due in part to increased awareness of potential birth complications...and to an increased tendency on the part of litigation-fearing doctors to opt for the safer more predictable course.

Premature babies have premature organs and can require medical assistance with vital functions like eating and breathing. Even babies born on time may be *jaundiced* (yellow color to skin and whites of eyes) as a result of immature liver function. Incompatibility between baby and mother's *Rh blood types* can lead to (treatable) problems at birth.

I GUESS MOMMY JUST ISN'T MY TYPE...

Arriving in this world safe and sound depends not only on baby's genetic endowment,

and on the ease (or difficulty) of childbirth,

but also on the environment into which she is born.

Many of those unfortunate enough to have been carried by pregnant mothers who took *thalidomide* during the 1950s (or *DES* in more recent years) were born with one or more serious birth defects.

WHOA!! I JUST HOPE I'M INSURED...

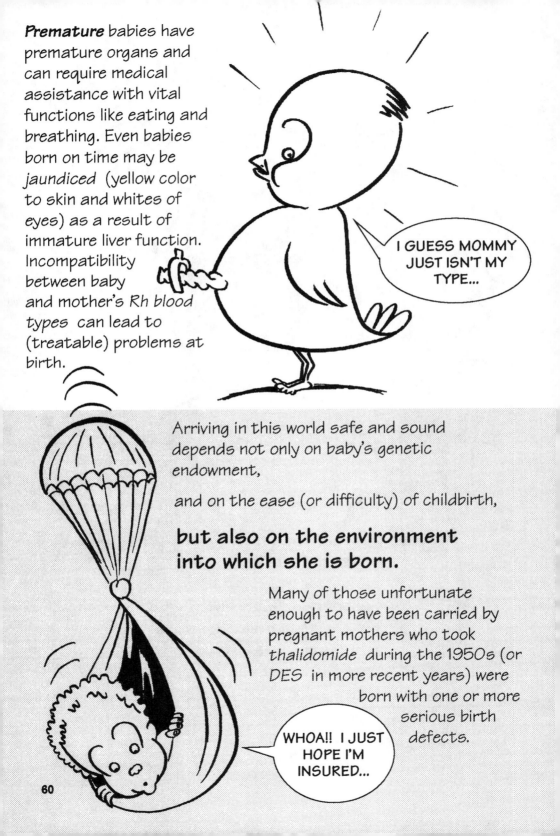

In developing countries, far too many babies—up to one fifth—weigh far too little—less than 5 1/2 pounds—at birth.

LET THEM EAT CAKE.

The usual cause of low birth weight is inadequate nutrition, which can result from insufficient calories, or not enough protein or vitamins and minerals.

BABY BASICS

**First-time parents can feel overwhelmed by doubt:
How much sleep does my baby need?
How often should she eat?**

Are we doing things right?

There is no one 'right' way.

Knowledge comes with practice.

The major task of the first few days is to help the baby get used to (extra-uterine) life. Babies need to be held frequently and closely and should be kept warm and clean. Newborns sleep much of the time, and take only small amounts of fluids...typically, there is some weight loss until the fourth or fifth day. When infants are tired they sleep...and when hungry, they will eat. At first, there may be no discernible pattern to the baby's eating and sleeping. Follow her cues. Eventually, with sensitive parental involvement and response, a definite rhythm will emerge.

OMB WITH A VIEW: Part II

For better or worse, parenting begins *before* birth.

Mother becomes aware of 'quickening'—fetal movements including kicking—before the fifth month.

AND there is now good evidence that unborn babies are aware too: aware of sound and movement and maybe even light.

So it may not be that far-fetched for parents to read or sing to baby through mom's belly— this may actually promote early recognition by baby of mom and dad's voices.

Some have argued in favor of **Pre-Natal Universities**—formalized educational programs for the unborn—based on findings that the fetus can learn.

Newborn babies seem to prefer sounds to which they were exposed prior to birth, including theme songs of soap operas viewed by their moms!...Some researchers believe that directed pre-natal stimulation may enhance learning, attachment and physical development of the infant.

Life After... BIRTH

Almost from the start, babies—including those yet to be born—seek out new experiences.

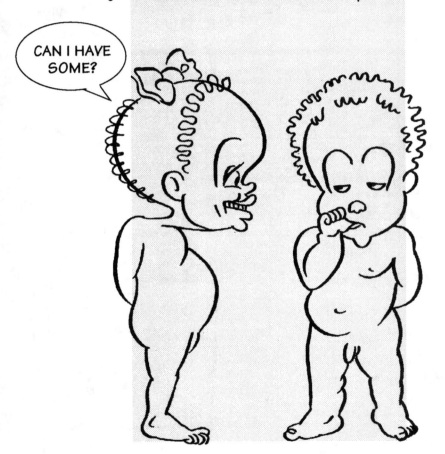

Babies relate to and attempt to control their environment. (Maybe this is why the fetus starts thumb sucking as early as four months: she is practicing an activity that will become extremely important to her later on when she wants to regulate the way she feels.)

The newborn's nervous system is programmed for automatic response (reflexes) as well as for growth and development (learning.)

Reflexes enable the newborn to carry out vital functions such as sucking (without choking), swallowing, and clinging to Mom and/or Dad.

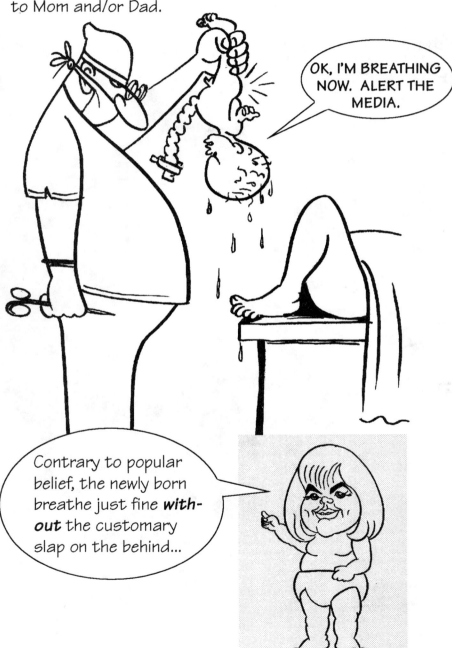

And that's not all.

The healthy newborn is highly competent, capable of a variety of behaviors ranging from initiating approach or avoidance movements to paying close attention to visual contrasts to expressing preference for her mother's voice over that of a stranger.

It's hard to say exactly *how* important input from the parents, other caretakers, and the environment is in shaping baby's behavior. (This kind of input is very difficult to measure.)

We do know that parental and environmental influences are crucial; but we also know that the newborn's timetable for growth and development is 'hard-wired' and will unfold all on its own (barring major interference), as the baby matures.

The plan is universal.

Rates of brain maturation and achievement of developmental milestones are identical across all cultures.

For instance: two day olds already pay selective and greater attention to their mothers' faces. At two to three weeks, babies open their mouths and stick out their tongues in what some have interpreted as a crude imitation of adult facial expressions.

NO SWEAT. I CAN DO THAT.

At the same time, mother is reacting to and stimulating the infant at the necessary pace.

YOU CALL THIS A DIALOGUE?

AM I CUTE? OR AM I CUTE?

Baby is already fascinated by and cueing into what is (and will remain) the most important aspect of her world:

people.

Babies, and newborns in particular, seem designed to elicit nurturing responses. By three months, babies are smiling regularly, and are especially responsive to the gaze of the mother or father.

These evolving behaviors all work toward maximizing baby's most immediately pressing task: **relatedness to parents and the world.**

BABY BASICS

Extra comfort, in the form of gentle rocking, singing, and/or wrapping the baby helps to soothe her and reassure her that she is in a safe and secure place. Bathing can also be a warm and welcome experience for the baby...or a negative one. Some babies prefer washcloth bathing—that's fine too. (A baby bath makes it easier to handle the infant's tiny body.)

With the maturation of her nervous system, baby's behavior and transactions become more complex. Babies become increasingly able to give and receive social signals.

Charles Darwin, who kept a journal of his own infant's development, was not alone in the belief that infants are to a certain extent capable of appreciating the feelings and intentions of those around them.

More recent studies suggest that infants and good mothers are highly *attuned* (aware of and responsive to) to each others' cues.

Lack of response on mother's part makes baby restless and anxious.

While the three month old appears equally comfortable with most any caretaker, the five month old shows an unmistakable preference for the mother (or other primary caretaker). Which is not to say that the primary caretaker has to be the mother; we know, from other cultures as well as our own, that other arrangements can and do work.

BABY BASICS

And then there's the diaper issue. Although cloth diapers don't pose the environmental hazard that disposables do, many parents feel that the smell hazard of dirty cloth diapers is far more immediate. Babies may not be aware of or may not particularly mind a wet or soiled diaper, so parents need to periodically check to see if it's time for a change.

Baby's diaper is most easily changed on a padded flat surface like a changing table.

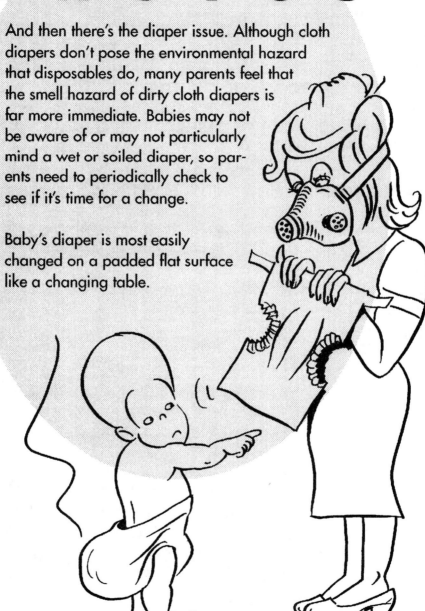

Meanwhile, back in Babyland...

> It's not just babies' behavior and emotions that change as they mature.

The infant also has a definite effect on the adults around her.

Amazingly enough, the infant comes into the world with a set of absolutely compelling social responses, not the least of which are her smile and her cry. As early as the second month, babies pay specific attention to **people**; sometime around the fourth month, indiscriminate smiling is replaced by selective smiling at people they know best.

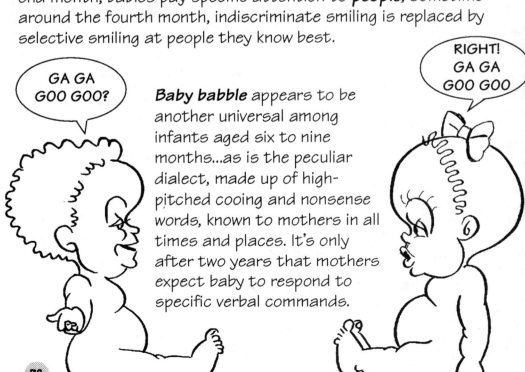

> GA GA GOO GOO?

Baby babble appears to be another universal among infants aged six to nine months...as is the peculiar dialect, made up of high-pitched cooing and nonsense words, known to mothers in all times and places. It's only after two years that mothers expect baby to respond to specific verbal commands.

> RIGHT! GA GA GOO GOO

We now know that there are real inborn differences among babies (so much for the old 'tabula rasa' [blank slate] notion of newborns.) There's a spectrum of baby personalities: some babies are timid by nature, others are very active, while others may be irritable and demanding.

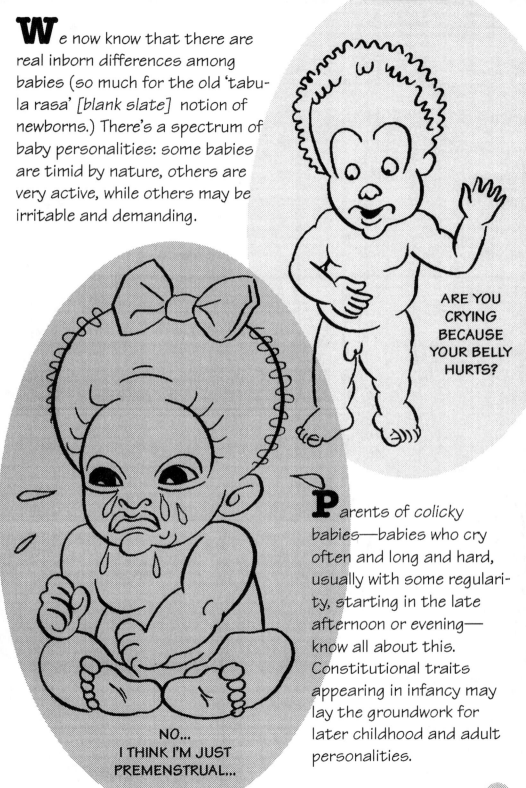

ARE YOU CRYING BECAUSE YOUR BELLY HURTS?

NO... I THINK I'M JUST PREMENSTRUAL...

Parents of colicky babies—babies who cry often and long and hard, usually with some regularity, starting in the late afternoon or evening—know all about this. Constitutional traits appearing in infancy may lay the groundwork for later childhood and adult personalities.

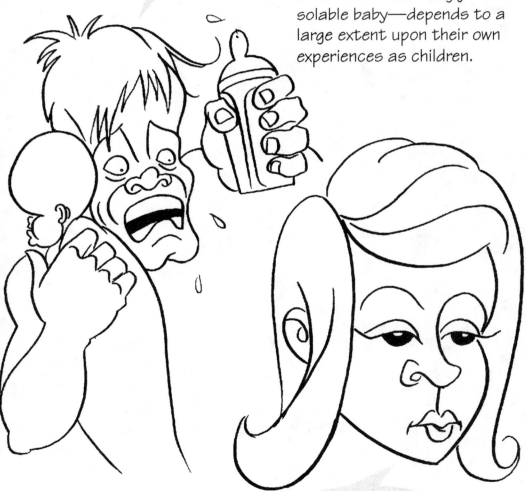

The parent-baby interaction is a *mutual* one, with each member of the pair shaping the other's response.

Parents' ability to soothe and comfort babies—to not get rattled in the face of an irritable and seemingly inconsolable baby—depends to a large extent upon their own experiences as children.

BABY BASICS

Breast or Bottle— Which is best?

The answer is: whatever's best for (the two or three of) you. Many babies and moms take to breast-feeding very readily...and some don't. The bottle vs. breast controversy is complicated by considerations of milk availability and life style (It may not always be convenient for mother to offer her breast.)

Some mothers work out a combined approach, alternating between breast milk and bottle. Baby formulas, though not identical to mother's milk (they lack mother's antibodies, which confer some immunological protection to baby), are adequate sources of comfort and nutrition. Nursing mothers need to be aware that most drugs they take will appear in the breast milk and will therefore be passed along to baby.

Formula is available in numerous varieties. Powdered or condensed formula require mixing with cooled boiled water. Other types are ready to use right from the can. In any case, baby's bottles and water (along with formula and mother's milk, babies like water from time to time) should be sterilized before use, since bacteria are everywhere and baby's immune system is not yet fully competent.

Baby's smile, which by three months has become one of baby's main modes of expression, lets the parents know that they are in touch, that baby is happy, that they are effective in caring for him.

I'M AFRAID YOU ONLY GET Bs THIS PAST MONTH...

Mothers who suffer from depression (including post-partum depression, which is an episode of severe depression that begins some time after the baby is born) are at risk of withdrawing emotionally from the infant.

Depression is common among lower socio-economic mothers of young children, particularly among women who are unemployed, have three or more children, and lack social supports.

> What shall I give my children?
>
> who are poor,
> Who are adjudged the least-
> wise of the land.
> —Gwendolyn Brooks,
> *Annie Allen* (1949)

BONDING
FOR BEGINNERS

Taking care of baby's physical needs—diet, hygiene, sleep schedule—is not enough. Infants can suffer *emotional* malnutrition.

Orphanage babies with too few opportunities for play, movement and human contact fail to grow, become ill, and even die. Maternal deprivation—absence of consistent and continuous mothering during the sensitive period between 6 and 36 months—can result in significant language and relationship difficulties in later life.

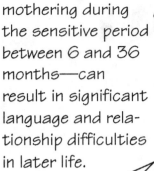

This has been a particularly critical issue for babies raised in institutions. Babies and chilren require social stimulation, interesting surroundings, and ongoing interaction with a highly responsive and sensitive primary caretaker—ideally, their mother.

BONDING CAN TAKE TIME.

Not uncommonly, fathers find themselves becoming more deeply involved as the infant becomes more aware of and responsive to him. While the mother-infant interaction has a number of consistent features from one culture to another, the father's role is more varied...

Fathers tend to be more playful and perhaps the less nurturing of the parent pair.

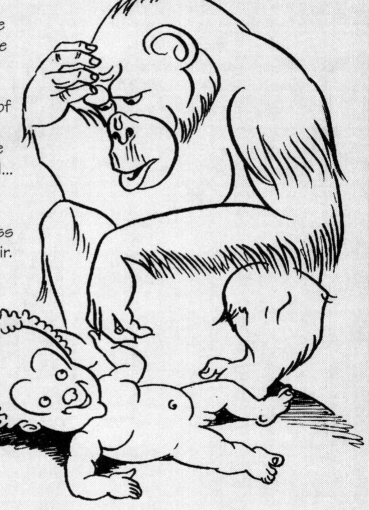

COME ON DAD YOU CAN CHANGE A DIAPER...

BABY BASICS

During feedings, babies swallow air. Lots of air. Which means they need time out during feedings in order to burp. Following a few gentle pats on the back, which usually suffices, the meal can be resumed. Baby dining is a dramatic, busy and colorful enterprise. Babies routinely spit up milk, or 'cheese' (partially digested stomach contents.) Occasionally they even vomit. Most often this is 'business as usual', but very frequent or forceful ('projectile') vomiting or vomiting in the presence of fever should be evaluated by a doctor.

From Baby Steps to...

Giant Steps

Babies' way of looking at the world and processing what they see (cognition) becomes increasingly sophisticated.

TODAY I MOVE MY THUMB TOMORROW THE WORLD!!

At first, the infant relates to his body haphazardly, as though it were part of the environment.

But gradually as he learns to lift his head, to use his hands to reach for things...he finds himself achieving greater and greater control over his world.

'GROWN-UPS FOR BEGINNERS':

Babies delight in having and mastering new experiences...

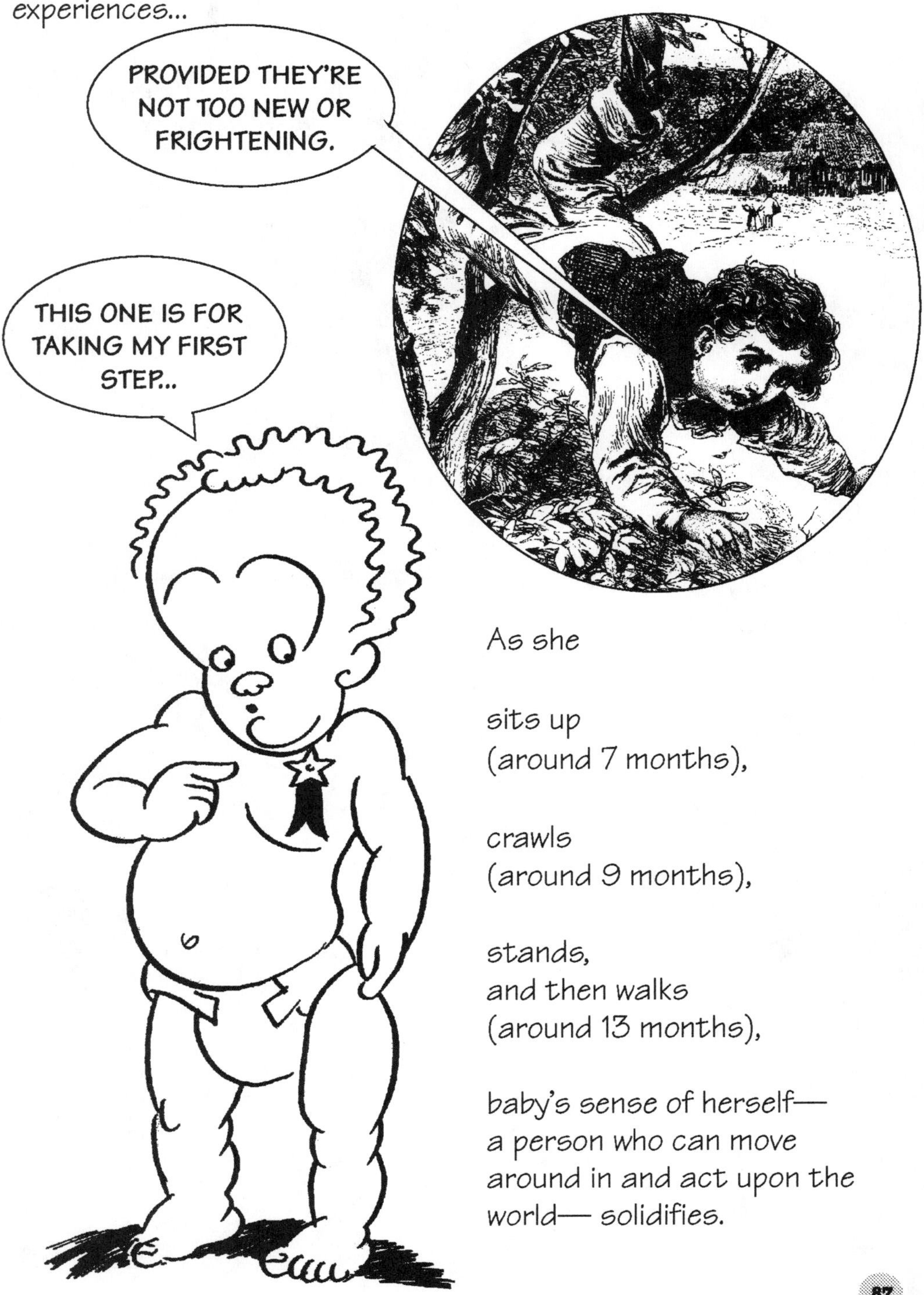

PROVIDED THEY'RE NOT TOO NEW OR FRIGHTENING.

THIS ONE IS FOR TAKING MY FIRST STEP...

As she

sits up
(around 7 months),

crawls
(around 9 months),

stands,
and then walks
(around 13 months),

baby's sense of herself—
a person who can move
around in and act upon the
world— solidifies.

Forming **attachments** to caretakers may be the main developmental task of the first six months.

It is likely that **basic trust** in the child results from the attentions of an indulgent loving mother.

(Advice of disciplinarians notwithstanding, it's actually very difficult to spoil an infant.)

One of the preludes to subsequent conversations is baby and parent's *joint attention* to an object.

Which of course is only the beginning.

Successful *differentiation* of self from not-self (12 to 18 months)—a sense that others are separate from them—leads to empathy and increased socialization.

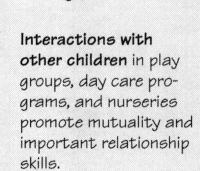

Interactions with other children in play groups, day care programs, and nurseries promote mutuality and important relationship skills.

Baby's later relationships will also depend on the quantity and quality of her early environment:

▶ How many people were involved in looking after her?

▶ How many separations and losses occurred?

▶ Were there brothers and sisters present, and if so, were they primary peers, competitors, or caretakers?

Collective monologue was how Jean Piaget described babies' first 'conversations.' Babies engage in 'parallel play'—they tolerate each others' presence, but are more are less self-involved when it comes to play.

Babies who grow up in stimulating environments that feature frequent conversation acquire language skills sooner.

Baby's speech progresses from simple one word utterances like Mama and Da-da to judgmental language (dirty, bad, good, not nice)...

which facilitates baby's self-evaluation, feelings of mastery or failure, shame, guilt...and growing sense of right and wrong.

MMMPH!

Words are not only a source of shame and guilt, but they can also be a powerful source of gratification. Children enjoy the sense of mastery and approval that comes from increased self-control and the ability to delay rewards.

GROWN-UPS FOR BEGINNERS:
Toilet training can be fun...or a living hell.

Parents may try to impose their own *tight-assed* values on unwitting babies...

Watch out!

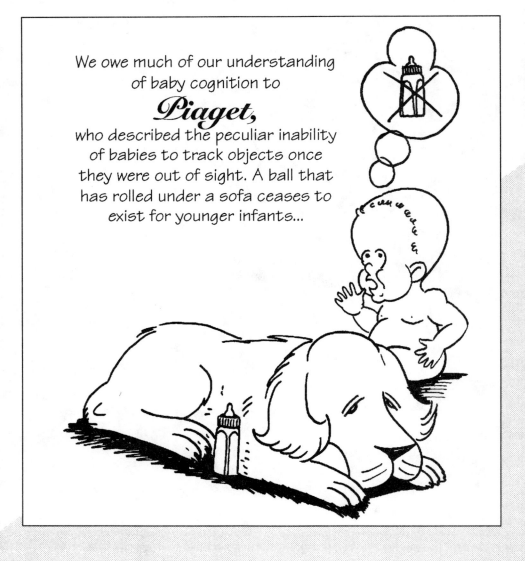

"Grown-ups never understand anything for themselves, and it is tiresome for children to be always and forever explaining to them."
—The Little Prince (1943)

Babies don't begin to achieve **object constancy** until 7 months, while babies' **separation anxiety** (at 8 months) and **'touching base'** (looking repeatedly at Mom while baby's at play) remain prominent until the baby can **internalize** the presence of her mother (second and third years.)

This is aided by the development of increasingly sophisticated speech, which by age two facilitates the child's interactions and liberates her (via her ability to name things and remember them at will) from the tyranny of the ever changing here-and-now.

TO 'PLAY IT OUT' IS THE MOST NATURAL SELF-HEALING METHOD CHILDHOOD AFFORDS.
—ERIK ERIKSON

By age three, children have an active fantasy life, and more and more engage in playing **'pretend.'**

They believe that adults always know what children are thinking.

And they believe that they are the cause of whatever happens around them.

So that the child blames herself for painful experiences like losses, separation, and violence in the home.

Baby's every achievement, from his or her first word to standing to walking, can be a source of pride for parents.

But parental expectations aside, most babies don't reach their milestones at the predicted time; and later abilities have little to do with how old the child was when she reached the milestone.

BABY MILESTONES

	Approximate age (months):
lifts head when on back	2
turns over	3-4
sits	6-10
stands while holding	10
walks	12-14
says 3 words	12-20
puts two words together	21

BABY BASICS

By four to six months, solid foods such as cereals and strained fruits and vegetables can be given. Certain items—strawberries, for example—can cause allergies in young babies, so parents should check before introducing any new foods. A high chair makes feeding baby easier, and establishes a kind of helpful ritual—mealtime is a special time devoted to...food!

By one year, most babies are ready for cow's milk. Weaning from breast or bottle should be done gradually, always using baby's comfort level as a cue. Feeding should be a pleasurable activity for all concerned, not an ordeal or a test of wills. (Food should *not* be used as a reward.) Doctors often recommend supplementing baby's diet with specific multiple vitamins.

Comparative Baby-Rearing

(For Beginners)

Although these growth stages are the same from one culture to another, parenting arrangements and parental response patterns definitely are not.

Compare for example the Navajo baby tightly cinched in to a cradleboard, or the Slavic baby, wrapped up in swaddling cloth, with their Western counterpart, who is left free to loll about...and on occasion, to cry.

Cross-cultural variation in baby-rearing includes practices like multiple caretaking (as in the traditional extended family, now on the wane), communal caretaking (as on the Israeli *kibbutz*), and day care (among single parent and working couple families in the West).

MOMMY?

No one has ever proven that one method is better than another.

BABY BASICS

BABIES GROW

Height and weight charts are available which help to determine whether or not baby is where he should be for his age.

BRUISES
FOR BEGINNERS...

Little Polly Flinders
Sat among the cinders,
Warming her pretty
   little toes.
Her mother came and
   caught her,
And whipped her little
   daughter
For spoiling her nice
   new clothes.
Little Polly Flinders

Antisocial behavior (aggression, stealing, truancy, drug use) is more common among impoverished and otherwise socioeconomically deprived children.

Who are in turn at greater risk of criminality in later life...

Obstacles to optimal growth and development like large family size, birth injury, and family mental illness and criminality are more prevalent among lower socioeconomic class children.

Class differences affect parental beliefs about child-rearing as well as parental behavior (lower class mothers are more likely to rely on corporal punishment.)

What happens in the home makes a deep and often indelible impression on young minds, casting the template for baby's own future relationships.

Serious conflict between Mom and Dad may lead to adjustment problems for their kids...with male children of divorce at greater risk of antisocial problems as adults.

Parents learn parenting styles early on...we tend to treat our children in much the same way that we ourselves were treated.

Which means, sad to say, that children who were victimized are likely to become abusers themselves.

BABY BASICS

Crying...
in infants, it's usually not for joy!

Babies cry for many reasons, including hunger, pain, irritability, and cold. Try your best to identify and correct the immediate cause. Beyond this, rocking the baby, allowing her to suck at a pacifier, singing to her, and wheeling her in a carriage are all effective anti-crying techniques.

That's right. According to one study, almost twenty per cent of baby deaths under age one in the U.S. (first half of the 1980s) resulted from homicide. The first six months are the peak period of childhood abuse.

O, neglectful nature, wherefore art thou thus partial, becoming to some of thy children a tender and benignant mother, to others a most cruel and ruthless stepmother? I see thy children given unto slavery to others without ever receiving any benefit, and in lieu of any reward for the services they have done for them they are repaid by the severest punishments.

—Leonardo da Vinci, *The Notebooks*

BABY BASICS

Teething, beginning after four months, is difficult for parents and painful for babies. Medicated gels should be avoided (the drugs in these are strong and can be absorbed through the gums into the body.)

Colicky babies, who mount screaming fits lasting from one to four hours on a regular daily basis, can be a real challenge...moms and dads need to resign themselves to the onslaught, secure in the knowledge that baby will eventually settle into a more livable peaceable schedule.

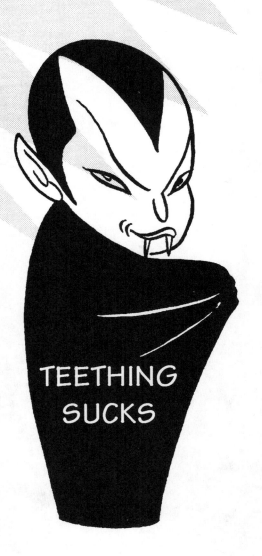

TEETHING SUCKS

'You Must Have Been A Beautiful [or Brilliant or Beastly] Baby'

No one has the exact recipe for an Einstein, or a Shakespeare, or a Qadaffi...and maybe it's better that we don't!

Claims of genetically determined differences in intelligence between races have not been verified.

Intelligence is inborn to a certain extent, but the influence of a child's environment can be enormous. Where educational opportunities are few and far between, inherited differences in intelligence will predominate.

The mother's level of education predicts tested abilities in infants as early as eighteen months of age...as does the amount and variety of stimulating experiences in the home.

AND school performance directly affects the child's mental health, with failure often going hand-in-hand with childhood conduct problems and then personality disorder in adulthood.

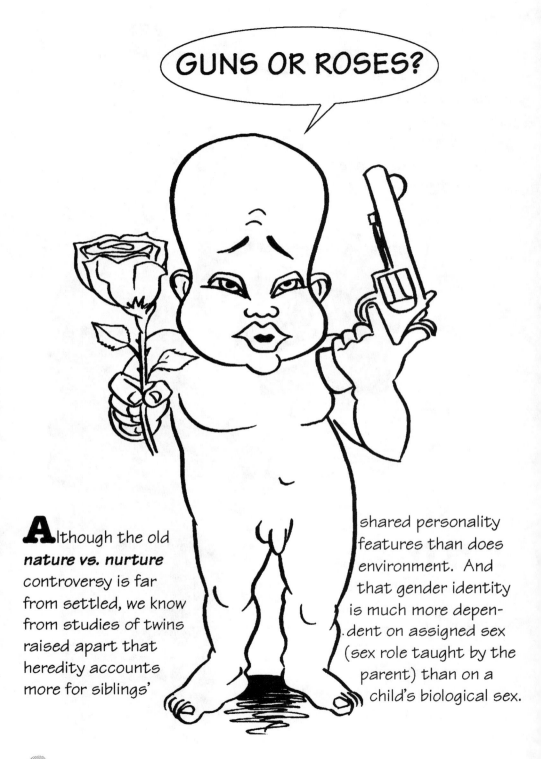

Although the old **nature vs. nurture** controversy is far from settled, we know from studies of twins raised apart that heredity accounts more for siblings' shared personality features than does environment. And that gender identity is much more dependent on assigned sex (sex role taught by the parent) than on a child's biological sex.

BABY BOYS FOR BEGINNERS:

Explain it as you like—but boys the world over are more aggressive than girls.

Role Models & Identification
(for Beginners)

There is also good evidence that sexual preference (homo- vs. heterosexuality) is determined from a very early age, and is evident in the child's choice of **role models** and of toys and manner of dress.

In Western societies, most children play with other children of the same sex.

Many believe that personality and sexual orientation are critically determined by the child's **identifications**: that is, which parent the child wants or for that matter definitely doesn't want to be like.

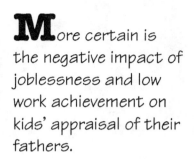

"MY DAD'S IN RESOURCE ALLOCATION..."

ore certain is the negative impact of joblessness and low work achievement on kids' appraisal of their fathers.

Following the U.S. economic Depression in 1929, the life adjustment of sons (whose primary identification is with their fathers) was impaired more than that of daughters.

And currently, in lower class households where there is no father, or where mothers denigrate men, boys are hard put to find healthy role models upon whom they can model their adult lives.

> Girls may have more difficulty than boys in achieving a solid identification with their same-sex parent, especially if you believe that girls compete with their moms (at least in their minds) for the attention of their dad.

BABY BASICS

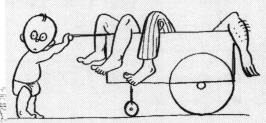

Entire books have been written about baby's sleep (or lack of.)

Tending 'night babies' can be an exhausting experience, particularly for moms and dads who have daytime responsibilities like jobs...

Strategy is key. Bedtime should not be used as a threat or punishment. Sleeping should be something for baby to look forward to. (Clever parents figure out how to smoothe baby's transition from waking to sleep. They also quickly learn to fall asleep as soon as baby has.)

Brothers (and Sisters) FOR BEGINNERS

Another big influence on personality is **birth order.**

First born children are often more confident than their brothers and sisters.

Reactions of children to the arrival of a new sibling can range from coolness to outright hostility.

THE FARTHER APART IN AGE, THE LESS LIKELY OR LESS INTENSE THE SIBLING RIVALRY.

Baby History

Seven years had long been considered the chronological limit of childhood; historically, this was the age beyond which children were expected to act (and work and even marry) as adults.

I HEAR THEY'RE HONEYMOONING IN DISNEY WORLD.

It wasn't until the seventeenth century, with the provision of children's clothing, age-specific schooling, and recreation, that this custom began to change.

BABY BASICS

It's the exceptional infant who can say, "Mom, I've got a stomach ache." Signs of illness in babies include fever, diminished eating or drinking, and excessive unexplained crying. Writing off a persistent change in baby's behavior as 'crankiness', or 'colic' should only be done *after* the possibility of medical illness has been convincingly ruled out.

Other 'immature' practices and beliefs have taken centuries for Europeans to outgrow...and some are still with us today.

Infanticide—the intentional murder of babies for superstitious or economic reasons—had for centuries been a regular feature of many cultures **(particularly for infant girls.)**

According to the doctrine of Original Sin, even *babies* could be fated to eternal damnation... with no hope that any environmental influence could be brought to bear to alter their [irredeemable] lives.

Hence the necessity to 'break' the child's will...

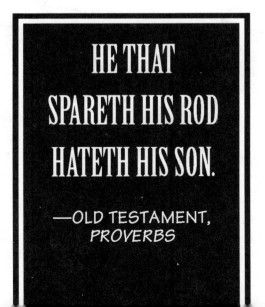

HE THAT SPARETH HIS ROD HATETH HIS SON.

—OLD TESTAMENT, PROVERBS

> There is now less flogging in the schools than formerly, but then less is learned there; so that what the boys get at one end they lose at the other.
> —Samuel Johnson (quoted in Boswell, 1775)

I'LL CALL YOU...

The decline of wet-nursing, and farming out of newborns and infants to surrogate mothers for a year or longer, coincides with the reduction in childbirth mortality and with the introduction (19th century) of baby bottles and formula.

Some 'modern' developments— like the Industrial Revolution— merely refined the types and amount of misery to which children could be exposed.

Seesaw, Margery Daw,
Jacky shall have a new master;
Jacky must have but a penny a day,
Because he can work no faster.
—Seesaw, Margery Daw

History has been written from the grown-ups' point of view. A second look at the wars and conquests and spread of civilizations—as they affected babies—might make each of us sit up...and cry.

BABY BASICS

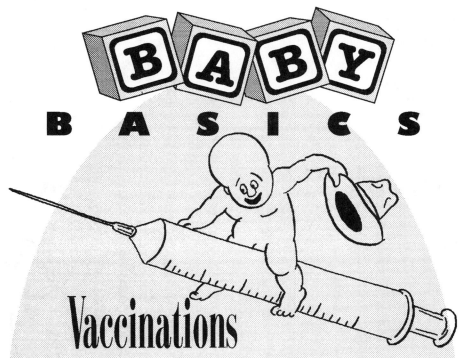

Vaccinations

	Recommended Age (months)
First oral polio	2
First DTP (diptheria, tetanus, whooping cough)	2
Second oral polio and DTP	4
Third DTP	6
Third oral polio	15
Fourth DTP	15
MMR (measles, mumps, rubella)	15
H influenza b	15
Oral polio and DTP	60

Teach Your Children

To help our babies grow to learn and to love, we have to do our best to understand and respect their needs. Child culture is based on concerns about helplessness and power...

> HERE! WALK A MILE IN <u>MY</u> SHOES.

and adults can do much to help or hinder these struggles of the young.

In silence I must take my seat...
I must not speak a useless word,
For children must be seen, not heard.
—B. W. Bellamy, *Open Sesame*

Human young have the longest childhood (weaning period) of all animal species...

and one reason for this may be that to become adults we have the most to learn.

BABY BASICS

Babies at play are a wonder.
Their endless fascination with things, with how things look and work and fit together, takes us back to when we were kids and the world was Playland...Through play, baby engages the world outside her and discovers how she can act upon it. Babies enjoy looking at and touching crib and stroller accessories like mirrors and mobiles. Providing stage-specific toys (i.e., rattlers and objects with strong visual contrasts for infants, puzzles and building blocks and crayons for older kids) promotes the child's growth through play.

The years following infancy are filled with physical, mental and some might even say spiritual changes.

"I DON'T WANT TO GROW UP..."
—PETER PAN

The child's moral sense, for example, progresses from a fixed set of beliefs (*grown-ups are always right, children and other people suffer because they are bad*) to a broader concern with what is fair and just.

Identifying the major influences on child development is only the first step. We also need to determine how and to what extent these influences can be modified to promote babies' (and therefore everyone else's) well-being.

THE CHILD IS FATHER OF THE MAN...
—WILLIAM WORDSWORTH (1807)

Children mimic parents. Parents who believe they can shape their lives pass this sense of confidence along to their kids.

Likewise, family tension and discord shows up all too often in the next generation (separation and/or divorce of warring parents can be a *positive* change in the child's life).

THE SINS OF THE FATHERS...

Babies need good mothering, as well as safe and secure and (mostly) predictable environments in which to grow and learn.

Children also need **other** children with whom they can play and test out their fledgling social skills.

BABY BASICS

Baby's environment should be a safe one. Baby's arrival transforms an ordinary home into a storehouse of potentially dangerous and even lethal objects (particularly true when the infant starts to crawl.)

Babyproofing includes removing sharp and breakable items like glassware from the reach of curious fingers; covering exposed electrical outlets and controls; and gating stairways and windows.

And then there's...
TV.

Like it or not, television is a steady companion for most children, who model their behavior, speech, and expectations of life on what they see on the tube.

If there is anything that we would wish to change in the child, we should examine it and see whether it is not something that could better be changed in ourselves.
—C.G. Jung

Grown-ups play make-believe too; they pretend that television violence is harmless, that it won't affect us.

Frustrated moms and dads often look to their children to succeed where they feel that they themselves have failed.

We can't form our children on our own concepts; we must take them and love them as God gives them to us.
—Goethe

BABY BASICS

Babies are totally dependent on their caretakers.
Some wonder if the parent's consistent availability and instantaneous responsiveness (to baby's hunger, to her tears, her babbling) can be excessive or over-indulgent.

Babies cannot be spoiled.

The total attention given to an infant establishes the foundations for the child's subsequent sense of security and confidence in herself.

Wise parents know how to enjoy baby's constant presence; most babies enjoy watching moms and dads shopping or cleaning or preparing a meal.

Kids should not have to meet parents' and teachers' unrealistic expectations, but should be provided with appropriate levels of challenge and stimulation. A child's self-esteem, her sense of being a capable, effective, and worthwhile person, is built on her experience of success.

Children begin by loving their parents; as they grow older they judge them; sometimes they forgive them.
—Oscar Wilde, *The Picture of Dorian Gray* (1891)

THE HELL WITH THIS!

Debate on whether or not mothers should remain at home during the day, breast-feed, or allow toddlers to sleep in their beds continues. (Working mothers may not have some of these options.)

BABY BASICS

Many parents don't have the luxury of staying at home with their babies.

Caretaking options—from day care to involvement of immediate family to hired help at home—need to be thoroughly investigated by parents with a view toward providing baby with the most consistent and stable situation possible. Moms and dads needn't feel guilty about their decision to work (or stay at home with baby.) Parents need to know that their child is left in safe, loving hands. Children exposed to multiple (good) caretakers early in life may be less shy than those solely dependent on mom or dad.

The baby perspective of history makes it clear that vast social changes are underway. Relatively fewer children experience the traditional mother-at-home-during-the-day-type family; more and more, both single and coupled parents of young children have to work.

> HURRY UP NOW DAD OR YOU'LL MISS THE BUS...

Adequate day care and formalized work leave need to be available as alternatives... unless we want a generation of 'latch-key' kids.

The need is especially acute in lower class environments, where pre-school programs like Head Start can make the difference between

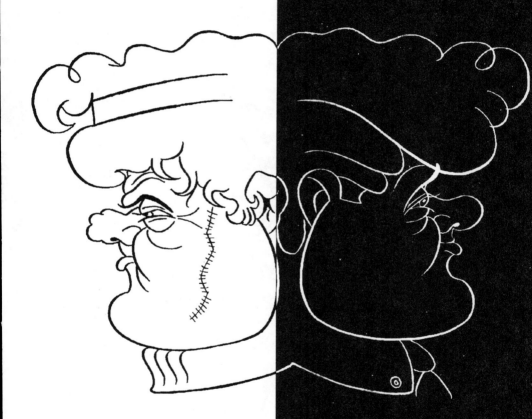

later delinquency or success.

BABY BASICS

And then there's the toddler.

The toddler, situated between infancy and childhood, now capable of unlimited movement and more than rudimentary speech, requires a skillful mix of flexibility and structure. She'll be wanting to try out new things—and she needs to, as long as she knows that mom or dad is watching. Toilet training comes up during this period, and is best approached in a relaxed and flexible way. The arrival of a second child offers the toddler an opportunity to be an older sibling, to test out her emerging selfhood in the presence of a new brother or sister.

Adequate prenatal care is necessary to reduce infant mortality rates.

Only 65% of black women and 60% of Native American women receive prenatal care, compared with 80% of white women.

Babies and children also need guaranteed access to quality health care.

Much of our highly-touted success in reducing infant and child mortality has resulted from improvement in *social* conditions like overcrowding, poor sanitation and poor nutrition.

The time has come for humanity to grow up, to own up to its responsibility not only to the planet but to the future generations who will live here:

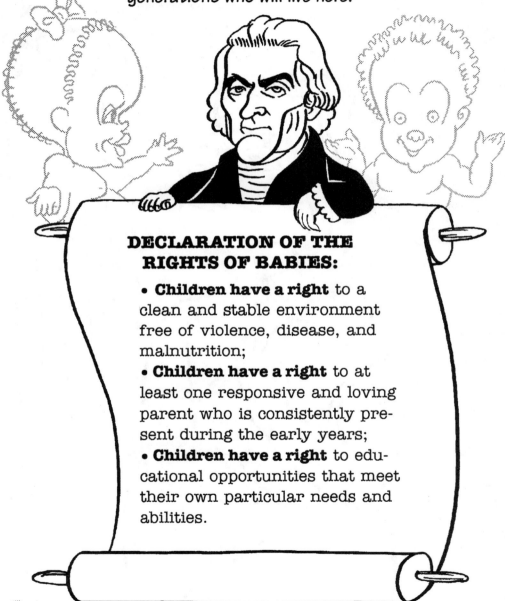

DECLARATION OF THE RIGHTS OF BABIES:

• **Children have a right** to a clean and stable environment free of violence, disease, and malnutrition;

• **Children have a right** to at least one responsive and loving parent who is consistently present during the early years;

• **Children have a right** to educational opportunities that meet their own particular needs and abilities.

Glossary

Abruptio Placentae: premature separation of the placenta from the wall of the uterus.

Amniocentesis: extraction of amniotic fluid by needle for prenatal diagnosis.

Amniotic Fluid: the fluid which surrounds the developing fetus in the womb.

Apgar Score: an overall health or viability score, from 0 to 10, assigned by doctors to the newborn.

Artificial Insemination: conception by means other than intercourse, such as *in vitro* (test tube) fertilization.

Blastocyst: the multi-celled precursor of both the embryo and the placenta.

Breech Presentation: bottom-, rather than headfirst, orientation of baby at the cervix.

Caesarian Section: surgical delivery of baby through a lower abdominal incision.

Cervix: anatomic structure leading from the uterus to the vagina.

Chromosomes: the genetic material inherited from both parents, made up of strands of DNA molecules, which provides the blueprint for the developing human.

Cognition: the faculty of perception, including memory.

Colic: a common disorder among infants marked by persistent spells of crying and distress. Its cause is unknown.

Collective Monologue: Dr. Jean Piaget's term for the non-conversational babble that babies make in each other's company.

Conception: creation of a new life via the fusion of the father's sperm and the mother's egg.

Congenital Malformation: a physical abnormality, such as a harelip or a port wine stain on the skin, already present at birth.

DES: diethylstilbestrol; a medication now implicated in fertility and other problems in children of mothers who previously received this.

DNA: deoxyribonucleic acid; the molecular building blocks of chromosomes. The specific DNA makeup determines the structure and function of an individual's body.

Ectopic Pregnancy: implantation and development of the embryo in a site other than the uterus. Can be life threatening.

Ejaculate: sperm plus seminal fluid, released from the penis as a result of orgasm.

Embryo: the developing human organism, from conception to two months.

Epidural: a narrow space outside the spinal cord in which medication such as anaesthetics can be administered.

Extrauterine: outside the uterus.

Fetal Alcohol Syndrome: serious disorders, including low birth weight, mental retardation, and cardiac abnormalities, which can appear in children born to alcoholic mothers.

Fetal Period: from two months to delivery.
Gamete: primary sex cell (male spermatozoon, female ovum.)
Genetic Engineering: intentional manipulation of the genetic material to alter the outcome of conception and development.
Inner Cell Mass: primordial group of cells that eventually gives rise to the embryo.
Internalization: a psychological process involving the 'taking in' or mimicking of various behaviors, attitudes, and values of another person.
Meconium: fetal waste matter; its appearance in the amniotic fluid, as determined by amniocentesis, can be a sign of fetal distress.
Nature vs. Nurture: a longstanding and still unsettled controversy; specifically, is heredity or environment more influential in determining the behavioral characteristics (such as personality and intelligence) in an individual?
Object Constancy: the child's developing ability to believe that something or someone continues to exist even when out of sight.
Ontogeny: the sequence of structural changes that take place in the developing embryo and fetus.
Ovum: female egg cell.
Ovulation: release of the ovum from the ovary; usually occurs once monthly in women of child-bearing age, and is a necessary precursor to conception.
Peristalsis: the regular and rhythmic contraction of involuntary muscles, such as those lining the intestine.
Phylogeny: the evolutionary sequence leading from the simplest one-celled organisms to higher (= more complex) organisms such as man.
Pitocin: (oxytocin): a hormone which stimulates uterine contraction. May be administered to hasten labor and delivery.
Placenta: embedded in the uterus, this tissue permits oxygen and nutrient and waste matter exchange between fetus and mother. Connected to the fetus and mother. Connected to the fetus by the umbilical cord.
Placenta Previa: placement of the placenta at or near the cervical opening of the uterus; can threaten the fetus' life-sustaining connection to the placenta.
Pre-eclampsia: a complication of pregnancy in which the previously healthy mother-to-be may develop hypertension, high blood sugar, and other medical problems.
Prenatal: before birth.
Procreation: creating life.
Quickening: fetal movements, such as kicking, which appear around the fifth month; usually noticed by the mother!
Separation Anxiety: anxiety or fear provoked in a child by separation or anticipated separation from a parent.

Sterilization: removal, by surgery or other means, of an individual's ability to reproduce.

Tabula Rasa: Latin for 'blank slate.' It was previously thought that infants came into the world completely unprogrammed; that their later personalities resulted from the environmental input they received during development.

Teratogenic: causing abnormalities in the developing embryo or fetus.

Testosterone: the presence or relative absence of this hormone is largely responsible for secondary sex characteristics such as hair distribution and aggression.

Toxemia (of pregnancy): pre-eclampsia.

Trimester: a three month period. Pregnancy is typically divided into three trimesters.

Ultrasonography: the use of sound waves to assess fetal health.

Umbilical Cord: a bundle of blood vessels and tissues that connects the fetus to the placenta (and therefore to the mother.)

Umbilical Cord Prolapse: a life-threatening condition in which the umbilical cord can literally strangle the emerging baby.

Uterus: (= the womb.) Female organ of reproduction, located in the lower abdomen, in which the placenta and embryo implant and develop.

Uterine: referring to the uterus.

Zygote: a cell resulting from the union of two sex cells.

References
(alphabetized by author)

Abt-Garrison History of Pediatrics, by Arthur F. Abt. Philadelphia, W.B. Saunders Company, 1965.

The Magic Years: Understanding and Handling the Problems of Early Childhood, by Selma Fraiberg. New York, Scribner, 1959.

Sex and Destiny: The Politics of Human Fertility, by Germaine Greer. New York, Harper Colophon Books, 1984.

Childhood: A Multicultural Perspective, by Melvin Konner. New York, Little Brown and Co., 1993.

Baby + Life: Help Your Child in a Life-Threatening Emergency. Learn What You Can Do to Prevent One from Happening, by Noel Merenstein (illustrations by Steve Biasi.) New York, Doubleday, 1990.

Dr. Spock's Baby and Child Care, by Benjamin Spock (6th edition.) New York, NAL-Dutton, 1992.

The Child's Conception of the World, by Jean Piaget. (Translated by Joan and Andrew Tomlinson.) Totowa, New Jersey, Littlefield, Adams, 1972.

The Interpersonal World of the Infant: A View from Psychoanalysis and Developmental Psychology, by Daniel N. Stern. New York, Basic Books, 1985.

Childhood & Human Nature: The Development of Personality, by Sula Wolff. London, Routledge, 1989.